A HISTORICAL ALBUM OF

KENTUCKY

A HISTORICAL ALBUM OF

KENTUCKY

Adam Smith ◆ Katherine Snow Smith

THE MILLBROOK PRESS, Brookfield, Connecticut

Front and back cover: "Oakland House and Race Course, Louisville," painting by Robert Brammer and Augustus A. Von Smith. Courtesy of the J. B. Speed Art Museum

Title page: Kentucky Derby. Courtesy of the Keeneland Association, Inc.

Library of Congress Cataloging-in-Publication Data

Adam Smith. 1965–
      A historical album of Kentucky / Adam and Katherine Snow Smith.
          p.   cm. — (Historical albums)
      Includes bibliographical references and index.
      Summary: A history of Kentucky, from its early exploration
and settlement to the state today.
      ISBN 1-56294-507-6 (lib. bdg.)   ISBN 1-56294-850-4 (pbk.)
      1. Kentucky—History—Juvenile literature. 2. Kentucky—
Gazetteers—Juvenile literature. I. Smith, Katherine Snow, 1968–. II. Title.
III. Series.
F451.3.S65 1995
976.9—dc20   94-39242
                                                                   CIP
                                                                    AC

 Created in association with Media Projects Incorporated

        C. Carter Smith, *Executive Editor*
        Lelia Wardwell, *Managing Editor*
        Adam Smith and Katherine Snow Smith, *Principal Writers*
        Bernard Schleifer, *Art Director*
        Shelley Latham, *Production Editor*
        Arlene Goldberg, *Cartographer*

Consultant: Betty Kelly Fugate, Kentucky Historical Society

Copyright © 1995 by The Millbrook Press, Inc.

Manufactured in the United States of America

10 9 8 7 6 5 4 3 2 1

CONTENTS

Introduction

Kentucky is a state of contrasts. Famous for its thoroughbred horses and prosperous tobacco farms, it is also plagued by extreme rural poverty in its Appalachian region. The state boasts great scenic beauty in its colorful woodlands, dramatic waterfalls and underground caves, yet it has also been scarred by careless land use, particularly in the manufacturing and coal mining industries.

It is a state that is both Northern and Southern in character, a state that was the birthplace of both the president of the Union during the Civil War (Abraham Lincoln) and the president of the Confederacy (Jefferson Davis). It was home to rugged mountain men best known for their bitter, violent feuding. And it produced some of American history's greatest statesmen and military leaders, people like Henry Clay and George Rogers Clark.

All this is Kentucky, the rugged territory that in colonial times served as gateway to America's western frontier. Thousands of years ago, prehistoric people made this land their home. After America became a nation, some of its bravest and most colorful figures pushed their way into this raw, unsettled territory. Clad in deerskin and armed with axes and long rifles, rugged adventurers like Daniel Boone journeyed into the wilderness and made communities out of often hostile surroundings, paving the way for an expanding America.

Since then, Kentucky has kept pace with the rest of the country, developing its abundant natural resources into many different successful industries. Coal, tobacco, and bourbon are three products for which Kentucky is famous, but the state has also become known for industries as diverse as automobile manufacturing and horse breeding. Today the state's rich historical heritage survives in such American institutions as the Kentucky Derby and bluegrass music.

PART ONE

OPENING THE FRONTIER

Long before settlers traveled to Kentucky by way of the Cumberland Trail, this natural path through the Allegheny Mountains was used by Native Americans as a trade route and war path.

In the late 1700s, Kentucky was considered the western frontier by settlers from the original thirteen colonies who wanted more land and more freedom. The Native Americans, however, did not want to give up their hunting grounds to a new surge of outsiders. The settlers fought many battles with the Native Americans and the British in their endeavor to establish permanent communities in Kentucky. In the end, the settlers prevailed, and in 1792, Kentucky was admitted to the Union as the fifteenth state. In the years that followed, Kentuckians worked hard to develop a fair government and a strong economy.

Traces of Prehistoric Life

Prehistoric people probably roamed what is now Kentucky as far back as 16,000 years ago. Archaeologists have found clues—broken bits of pottery, arrowheads, traces of dwellings and burial sites—that speak of how these people lived.

Kentucky's prehistory consists of six different civilizations. The earliest groups lived by hunting, using the area's many caves and overhanging cliffs for shelter. Game was plentiful: Large prehistoric mammals like mastodons and mammoths, creatures much larger than today's elephants, roamed the open, grassy plains.

The earliest people in Kentucky were the Paleo Indians, who lived from about 13,000 to 6000 BC. Archaeologists have found stone points from spears which the Paleo Indians used in hunting. The next group was the Archaic Culture, believed to dominate the area from 6000 to 1000 BC. They spent part of the year moving around but primarily they settled along the banks of Kentucky's many rivers, living off mussels and fish from the water.

The Woodland people, who lived from 1000 BC to AD 900, were probably the first Native Americans in Kentucky to practice farming. They hunted and fished, but also grew crops such as sunflowers, squash, and ragweed. Because the Woodland tribes had to stay near the crops until harvest time, they did not wander as much as the older cultures. They still traveled through the area in order to hunt. Along with spears, the Woodland people probably used the bow and arrow.

The Adena Culture overlapped with the Woodland Culture, occupying the area from 800 BC to AD 800 The Adenas grew even more crops than the Woodlands, eventually living in permanent villages near their fields. Adena settlements consisted of groups of small, round houses with cone-shaped roofs. The Adenas are believed to be the first group in Kentucky to make pottery. They also made jewelry from mica and copper, traces of which have been found in parts of the state.

The Mississippians, who lived from AD 1000 to AD 1600, added beans and corn to the farm crops grown by the Adenas. The Mississippians' way of farming was more advanced, and they used more sophisticated planting tools such as picks and hoes. Mississippian villages were bigger, with houses made from mud and straw.

At about the same time, from about 1200 to 1650, the Fort Ancient Culture lived in the Kentucky region. Their houses were rectangle-shaped and large. This group was skilled with the bow and arrow, and added wild birds and game to their diet of plants and fish. Archaeologists have discovered European tools alongside Fort Ancient artifacts, possible evidence that the Fort Ancient people may have traded with European explorers.

Other tribes came to Kentucky to hunt, returning to their homelands following the hunting season. These groups included the Cherokees and Chickasaws from the Tennessee Valley and farther south, and the Wyandottes, Delawares, and Shawnees from north of the Ohio River region. The Iroquois from New York also spent time in Kentucky, and were the ones to give the region its name: Kenta-ke. The English translation is not known for sure, but theories include "place of great meadows" or "land of tomorrow."

As different tribes came to the area, they competed for Kentucky's resources, sometimes fighting each other. In the 1600s they began to encounter a completely new kind of visitor: the European explorer.

The Fort Ancient Culture made pottery with detailed carvings, often resembling birds and animals. This ceramic pipe (above, right), carved in the form of a turkey buzzard, was used in religious ceremonies.

The Shawnees were one of the first tribes to live in the Kentucky region. Shawnee women (right) were an important part of the town government. Women chiefs directed the planting of crops, supervised feasts, and held the power to stop planned war raids.

Explorers Claim Kentucky

Europeans started coming to America, known as "the New World," in the 1620s. The first settlers built their homes and villages along the Atlantic Coast. By the late 1600s, settlers in the Carolinas and Virginia began to think about the land that lay west of the Appalachian Mountains.

The French had laid claim to large tracts of land in this region, but England was also very interested in expanding its American settlements westward. In 1654, an English colonel, Abram Wood of Virginia, made the first recorded visit to what is now Kentucky.

In the following decades, other explorers from both France and England passed through the area on trips down the Ohio River. In 1671, Robert Fallam and Thomas Batts of Virginia reached a divide along the New River and sent back reports about the rushing waters of the Ohio River.

A French expedition in 1750 tried to claim land for the king of France by leaving lead plates along a river that passed through Kentucky. But Britain tended to disregard such claims. That same year Thomas Walker led a group called the Loyal Land Company of Virginia on an exploration through the Kentucky region. He followed trails along the mountains, crossed the New River, then came to some very high rocky mountains too steep to climb over. The group traveled alongside the mountains for several miles to the east until they found a narrow opening between the steep rock walls. Walker named the opening after the Duke of Cumberland, and it became known as the Cumberland Gap. The Cumberland Gap was a monumental discovery: It was the meeting place for Kentucky, Tennessee, and Virginia, and in only a few decades the passageway would be the major entry point for many more explorers and settlers coming into Kentucky.

Although many early explorers came back with tales of rough terrain and hostile natives, it was not enough to stop Daniel Boone from planning a settlement in the West. Boone, an explorer who had already traveled much of the East Coast, first heard about Kentucky from a hunter, John Findley, who had been there. In 1769, Findley took Boone over the mountains through the Cumberland Gap into Kentucky. Boone spent two years exploring the wilderness on the other side of the mountains and hunting game there.

Meanwhile, his wife Rebecca waited at home, tending the crops and taking care of their children. When Boone finally returned to his family he told them that he wanted to one day live in the "second paradise" known as Kentucky.

Frontiersman John Findley (right) was a fur trader who first learned of the Cumberland Gap in 1752 from his Shawnee captors. He later guided Daniel Boone's first expedition along the trail to the Kentucky River.

Following his first trip to Kentucky, Daniel Boone described this land of rivers and mountains as a "second paradise." This 1849 painting (below) is titled Boone's "First View of Kentucky."

Settling an Untamed Land

The frontiersmen who first settled in Kentucky were brave and strong-willed, carving a life out of the wilderness in spite of many obstacles. Once they made the long journey by horseback or foot, they had a great deal of work to do to make a home in the wilderness: building log cabins, planting crops, and hunting bears, deer, and wild turkeys in the forest. The settlers lived in constant fear of attacks by neighboring Indians, who resented sharing their hunting grounds with the newcomers. In an effort to scare the settlers off, the Native Americans launched constant violent assaults against them.

In September 1773, the Boones and six other families set out to start what they believed to be the first settlement in Kentucky. Boone traveled with his wife, while his oldest son, James, trailed behind with a group of other youngsters. Two weeks into the journey, James and his friends were attacked by a band of Cherokees, and James and another child were killed. Despite his loss, Boone was determined to press on into Kentucky, but the other families, frightened by the attack, persuaded him to turn back. Boone lost his dream of being the first to settle in Kentucky when James Harrod established Harrodsburg, the first permanent settlement, in 1774.

But Boone did not give up. The Transylvania Land Company, a group from North Carolina, wanted him to start a settlement for them in Kentucky. Their leader, Judge Richard Henderson, signed a treaty with the Cherokee tribe in 1775 granting the company rights to Cherokee hunting grounds in Kentucky. Henderson hoped that a treaty and payment for the land would prevent later conflicts when the settlers moved in.

In exchange for the land, the 1,200 Cherokees at the treaty-signing ceremony at Sycamore Shoals received large supplies of animal furs, corn, ribbons, liquor, flour, trinkets, guns, ammunition, clothing, and tools. One Cherokee leader named Dragging Canoe thought his people were being cheated and shouldn't give up their hunting lands. He told Henderson that his effort to settle the land would be "dark and bloody." Both parties agreed to sign the treaty, but Dragging Canoe's prediction later turned out to be true.

In March 1775, Boone and twenty-nine other men set out to make a trail across the Cumberland Gap and find a place to settle. They burned down trees and cleared a path (which would later be widened to allow wagons to pass through). Along the way, Native Americans killed two members of the troop, Captain William Twetty and his slave.

It was the first sign that not all of the Cherokees recognized the treaty. However, Boone was determined to push forward. He picked a site along the Kentucky River where the group quickly built crude log cabins.

They next constructed a fortress around the cabins to protect them from attacks. The cabins were right beside each other in four rows, forming a rectangle, with walls joining the cabins on all sides. If necessary, the settlers could fight off Indian attacks from inside the fortress. Also, they could go to each others' homes without having to go out into the open.

Many of the men brought slaves with them. Back east, these slaves had worked on farms and plantations. The slaves played an important role in settling the wild Kentucky frontier. Side by side with the frontiersmen, they cleared paths, chopped down trees, built cabins, and planted crops.

A few months after the fortress, Boonesborough, was completed, the frontiersmen's wives and children arrived. The women began gathering and storing supplies for the coming winter. They spun yarn and wove it into blankets and made soap and candles out of animal fats.

Children's chores included gathering nuts, berries, and herbs from the forest. Women used the herbs and roots to make medicine and tea.

Frontier children were also responsible for watching the crops and scaring away birds that tried to eat the corn or scratch seeds out of the soil.

On July 14, 1776, Shawnees kidnapped Daniel Boone's daughter, Jemima, and Colonel Richard Calloway's daughters, Betsey and Frances, while they were canoeing on a river near Boonesborough. As the Native Americans dragged the girls toward their village, Betsey broke off tree branches and dropped torn-off scraps of her clothes to leave a trail for their rescuers.

Boone and nine men found the trail and caught up with the girls and their captors. The Shawnees released the prisoners unharmed and ran away. Two members of the rescue party later married two of the girls: Samuel Henderson married Betsey Calloway, and Flanders Calloway married Jemima Boone.

With all the challenges of the wild frontier, the settlers did their best to lead prosperous and happy lives. By 1776, more than 900 claims for land had been registered with the Transylvania Land Company, for a total of 560,000 acres. Thousands of settlers had poured into Kentucky. But a conflict arose when the Virginia Assembly claimed that some of the land that Henderson's land company was selling already belonged to Virginia.

Henderson, afraid he was going to lose rights to the land, organized an assembly of his own with representatives from Boonesborough and other forts. He wanted them to form their own state, with him as their leader. Most of the settlers, especially George Rogers Clark of Harrodsburg, didn't want to give up their freedom to Henderson. Clark convinced the Virginia Assembly and its governor, Patrick Henry, to make Kentucky a county of Virginia. As members of an official county, the people of Kentucky could be more involved in the government. Also, Virginia would provide them with financial and military support.

Clark had proven he was a valuable negotiator for Kentucky. He would also play an important role—for Kentucky as well as for the American colonies—as a military leader in the Revolutionary War.

Settlers used timber from Kentucky's forests to build sturdy log cabins, such as the one shown in this engraving (opposite, top). Usually made from pine or spruce logs, these simple, one-room houses could be built quickly by a group of neighbors and required no nails, which were almost impossible to get on the frontier.

Indian attacks on Kentucky settlements were frequent. In 1776, Jemima Boone and Betsey and Frances Calloway were kidnapped by Shawnees while canoeing on the river near Boonesborough. This 19th-century engraving (right) is a dramatic, if inaccurate, illustration of the scene. The girls were rescued and returned unharmed.

Kentucky During the Revolution

While Kentuckians were struggling for a hold on the rugged frontier, the original thirteen colonies were fighting the Revolutionary War against Britain. On July 4, 1776, the colonists had officially separated from Britain by signing the Declaration of Independence. Britain responded by sending troops to subdue the colonies, and the American Revolution was underway.

Most of the fighting took place within the original colonies. Some men left their homesteads in Kentucky and went east to join George Washington's army. The families left behind were vulnerable to attacks by Native Americans. Hoping to weaken the American cause, Britain gave some tribes weapons and sent military leaders to encourage them to attack the settlements. Britain hoped that once Kentucky soldiers heard there was trouble at home, they would desert Washington's army and return to protect their families.

The frontier families left their settlements and moved into forts, such as Boonesborough and Harrodsburg, for protection from attacks. Although most Kentuckians supported the Revolution, many men stayed home to defend the forts.

Britain's alliance with local Indian tribes was particularly dangerous for Boonesborough, the target of many attacks. Boonesborough residents hoped that heavy snowfall in the winter of 1778 would keep the Native Americans away, but Britain was planning another assault.

Because the pioneers were afraid of being attacked while tending the fields, Boonesborough's larders soon became empty—there was no bread, vegetables, or fruit. The settlers were existing on a meager diet of meat and water. Daniel Boone and a troop of men traveled several miles to the settlement of Blue Licks to collect salt in order to preserve meat. While there, Boone was ambushed and held captive by a group of Shawnees. They wanted him to lead them to Boonesborough so they could attack the settlement.

But Boone quickly thought up a plan. He advised the Indians not to attack the settlement in the middle of winter, when everyone was inside the fort and well-protected. He suggested waiting until spring when the people would be out working in the fields and much easier to capture. Boone's secret plan was to give his people several months to prepare for the attack by gathering ammunition and food. Boone and the other salt collectors were taken back to the Shawnee's camp and held prisoner while the Indians waited until spring to attack Boonesborough.

The Shawnees were very impressed with the frontiersmen's bravery and adopted a number of them into the tribe. The chief, Black Fish, soon loved Boone like a son and gave him a Shawnee name, Sheltowee. In early June Boone overheard Black Fish saying the British would offer them supplies to attack Boonesborough. Boone realized that he had to escape and warn his people.

Four days later, Boone reached Boonesborough after covering 160 miles of wilderness on foot. Once there he set to work preparing the fort for battle: The settlers quickly reinforced the walls of the fort, brought the animals inside, and prepared their weapons. Then they waited. It took the Shawnees longer to come than Boone had thought— so long that some of the untrusting Boonesborough settlers thought Boone had made it all up.

But in early September 1778, about 450 Shawnee warriors, dressed in war paint and bright feathers, approached the fort. They brought forty horses

In 1777, Boonesborough was transformed into a strong fort (above, right), enclosed by a ten-foot-high fence, when attacks on the settlement by neighboring Indian tribes became more frequent. In 1778, Shawnees fired at Boonesborough for nine days, but the fort protected the settlers until the Indians retreated.

This Shawnee warrior (right) is pictured wearing bright war paint, worn along with feathers during attacks. Prisoners captured by the warriors were either killed or adopted into the tribe to replace dead relatives.

with them to carry the women and children off as prisoners. The fighting lasted for several days. The settlers and the Shawnees fired back and forth at each other from the woods and the fort, fighting both day and night. Inside the fort, supplies of gun powder, food, and water were running low. Heavy rains fell and turned the ground to mud.

Outside Boonesborough the Shawnees were also cold, tired, and impatient. Not realizing how poor the conditions had become inside the fort, they decided the settlers would never surrender. After a nine-day seige, the Shawnees finally gave up and left. As soon as the siege ended, Boone journeyed to North Carolina where his family had taken refuge after his capture.

Although Boonesborough had won its safety, the rest of the Kentucky frontier was still vulnerable to the British and their Native American allies. Earlier in 1778, George Rogers Clark had gone from Harrodsburg to Virginia to request permission to form an army to attack British-led Indian troops in the Ohio area north of Kentucky. He persuaded Virginia governor Patrick Henry to give him ammunition and boats. He also got approval to offer each new recruit 300 acres of land in the conquered territory. Clark himself was named lieutenant colonel of the new force.

On Clark's return, he traveled through Pennsylvania to recruit troops, but most men were reluctant to leave their families unprotected. Back home, Clark managed to enlist only twenty-one men from Kentucky because so many were needed to protect the forts and settlements. By May 1778, Clark had managed to gather a small army of 350 men. In June, the army set out in canoes to fight the British. They successfully captured Kaskaskia and Vincennes, areas to the north that are now part of Illinois and Indiana.

Although the British surrendered to American and French forces at Yorktown, Virginia, in 1781, some fighting continued until a peace treaty was signed two years later. In August 1782, a force of several hundred Native Americans led by British captain William Caldwell attacked Bryan Station, a settlement near Boonesborough. The camp was so outnumbered that even women and children helped fight until reinforcements arrived from nearby camps. Caldwell, fearing that still more reinforcements would come, ordered his men and the Indian forces to retreat.

The settlers, confident of their victory, decided to go after the retreating warriors. This fateful decision resulted in the Battle of Blue Licks, one of the bloodiest battles against the Native Americans in Kentucky, but also one of the last. Daniel Boone urged the settlers to wait for more help before chasing down Caldwell's forces, but they were too anxious for revenge. The settlers caught up with the enemy at Blue Licks, where Boone had been taken captive a few

Simon Kenton (opposite) was a legend among frontiersmen. Captured by Native Americans in 1778, he was tied to the bare back of a wild colt, forced to run the gauntlet between two rows of club-swinging tribesmen, and tied to the stake three times before managing to escape back to Kentucky.

George Rogers Clark (above) devoted his career to the westward expansion of the United States. He was responsible for the protection of western settlements during the British-sponsored Indian raids on Kentucky during the Revolutionary War.

years earlier. The settlers were badly outnumbered, and sixty were killed.

News of the battle spread quickly throughout Kentucky, and hundreds of settlers from all over the area hurried in to help. With so many fighters on the way, the British and Native Americans fled back across the Ohio River.

On the Frontier of a New Republic

A new phase in Kentucky's life began when America and Britain signed a peace treaty in 1783 recognizing the independence of the states. The fighting days in Kentucky were finally over: British troops left the frontier, and most Native Americans caused little or no trouble for the settlers.

Following the Revolution, Kentucky was still considered a county of Virginia. In 1784, local leaders called the first of ten conventions for the people to discuss Kentucky's future. Some wanted Kentucky to remain part of Virginia, some wanted it to become a separate state, and some wanted Kentucky to be its own independent country. Statehood won out in the end, and in 1792 Kentucky became the fifteenth state to join the Union. At the first official session of the state legislature, leaders named the town of Frankfort Kentucky's permanent capital and home of the state government.

Kentucky leaders were also busy discussing a state constitution that included many points also in the Bill of Rights, such as freedom of religion, freedom of speech, and freedom of the press. The state government was set up with three branches: executive, legislative, and judicial. The constitution gave all males above the age of twenty-one, including free blacks, the right to vote in state elections.

Kentuckians had mixed feelings about slavery and the rights of African Americans. Slaves had been a part of Kentucky since the first slave-owning settlers came to the frontier. Some farms were so large that owners believed they needed slaves to grow and harvest the crops. However, many people in the state were opposed to slavery. In 1789, state leaders decided that foreign slaves in Kentucky would be considered free men and women. Slavery within the state would remain legal, however.

Eleven of the writers of the constitution in Kentucky were ministers and opponents of slavery. To prevent them from trying to overturn the decision, a clause was added to the constitution that ruled that ministers

All different kinds of leaders came together to achieve statehood for Kentucky. Shown opposite are the signatures of Thomas Walker, Daniel Boone, Simon Kenton, George Rogers Clark, Christopher Gist, George Washington, and Patrick Henry, collected from several documents relating to Kentucky's official admittance to the Union.

Revival meetings, such as this one (above), were religious as well as social functions. Entire families would attend, dividing their time between praying and socializing with old friends.

could not hold public office while serving in a church.

Religious leaders played a key role in shaping Kentucky's history, however. A period known as the Great Revival swept through Kentucky shortly before the start of the 19th century. Spirited religious meetings were held throughout the state, drawing huge crowds who came to hear the preachers, known as evangelists. Sometimes as many as 2,000 people came, bringing enough supplies to stay for an entire week of listening to sermons and sharing fellowship.

This was also a time of political debate, as Kentucky, along with the new nation, grappled with controversial issues. One of the most heated debates concerned the authority of the individual states versus the power of the federal government. Many Kentuckians considered themselves antifederalist, meaning that they believed each state had its own authority that was not completely subject to the federal government.

This issue came to a head in 1798 when the U.S. Congress passed the Alien and Sedition Acts, or "citizen acts," giving the federal government power to restrict the rights of foreigners and new citizens. Many Kentuckians opposed these laws, arguing that they were unfair to foreigners who wanted to become American citizens. Vice President Thomas Jefferson drafted a document for Kentuckians declaring the acts unconstitutional. James Madison did the same for

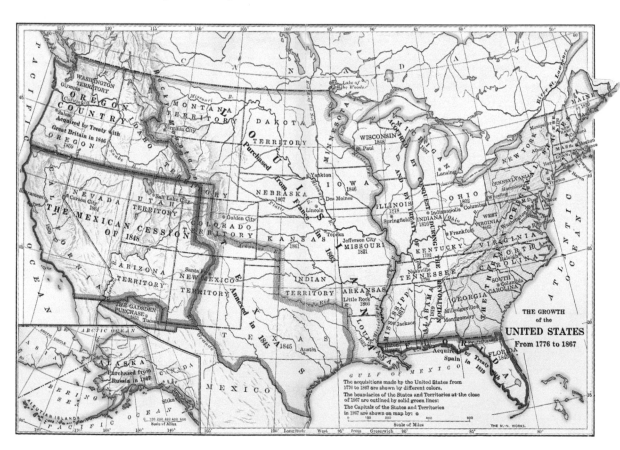

Virginia, and together the documents became known as the Kentucky and Virginia Resolutions. Both state legislatures adopted the resolutions to protest the Alien and Sedition Acts.

Jefferson again gained popularity with Kentuckians when he negotiated the Louisiana Purchase with France in 1803, assuring Kentucky and other states access to the Mississippi River. Kentucky in particular depended on the river as a trade route.

Another celebrated political hero in Kentucky was Henry Clay, a brilliant and powerful speaker. Clay was elected to the Kentucky state legislature in 1803. He was so popular that the people sent him to represent Kentucky in the U.S. Senate in 1806, when he was only twenty-nine. Clay was named Speaker of the House when he won election to the U.S. House of Representatives in 1811.

During Clay's terms in Congress, tensions between America and Britain began to build. Clay was one of several leaders from the West known as "war hawks," supporters of another war with Britain. The war hawks got their wish: One year after Clay's election to Congress, Britain and America were fighting the War of 1812. Thousands of Kentuckians, inspired by Clay's stand, signed up to fight on the American side. As many as 1,200 Kentuckians alone fought at the Battle of New Orleans in 1815, in which General Andrew Jackson led the American army to victory.

The United States acquired Louisiana from the French in 1803 when Thomas Jefferson negotiated the Louisiana Purchase (opposite). This purchase gave the United States control of the Mississippi River and allowed states, such as Kentucky, access to it for shipping goods.

During the War of 1812 between the Americans and British, about 5,500 Kentuckians fought in the Battle of New Orleans. General Andrew Jackson (above) led the Americans to victory and was considered a great hero throughout the country.

Stability and Growth

The early decades of the 19th century held many new developments for the state of Kentucky. The state continued to grow: More and more people were moving in, building Kentucky's economy and making advances in transportation. Political parties were gaining power as Kentuckians began playing a bigger role in the nation's government.

Slavery continued to be a disputed practice in the state. Most people in the South were proslavery. Other states had larger plantations than Kentucky and their economies depended on slavery to grow and harvest such cash crops as tobacco and cotton. In Kentucky, most farmers worked on smaller plots and were less dependent on slaves. Even so, some Kentucky farmers were slave owners and supported the system. Other Kentuckians who had come from the Carolinas, Virginia, and Tennessee, felt loyalties to the slaveholding states.

People who spoke out against slavery were known as abolitionists. Cassius M. Clay, a famous Kentucky antislavery leader, published a newspaper called *The True American* in Lexington in 1845. The paper's antislavery articles so angered supporters of slavery that they attacked Clay's offices. Clay was finally forced to move the paper to Cincinnati, Ohio.

The slavery debate raged across the country. In Congress, another Clay, named Henry, came to be known as the Great Compromiser. He tried several times to pull together both sides of the slavery issue. In 1820, Missouri wanted to be admitted to the Union as a slave state, where slavery would be legal. At that time America had eleven "free" states, forbidding slavery, and eleven slave states. Antislavery politicians feared that letting Missouri in as a slave state would upset the balance in Congress. To resolve the conflict, Clay proposed what came to be called the Missouri Compromise. Missouri could join the Union as a slave state if Maine, which had also just applied for statehood, could be admitted as a free state.

Clay ran for president in 1824 in a four-way race that was so close it had to be decided in the House of Representatives. Many expected Clay to win, but Clay gave his support to John Quincy Adams, thus winning him the presidency. In turn, Adams named Clay his secretary of state. Together they formed the Whig Party.

Clay's chief rival through much of his political career was Andrew Jackson, a popular war hero who became president in 1828, defeating Adams.

With the support of the Whigs, Clay tried twice more for the presidency, both times unsuccessfully. In 1832, Clay ran against Jackson's reelection effort and lost. He ran yet again as a Whig in 1844 and lost to

This 19th-century engraving (above) shows slaves being "sold down the river"—loaded onto steamboats for shipment down the Mississippi River to be auctioned off at Southern slave markets.

Cassius Marcellus Clay (right), son of a slave-holding planter, was an outspoken abolitionist and publisher of an antislavery newspaper in Lexington called *The True American*. The publication was eventually shut down by an angry proslavery mob.

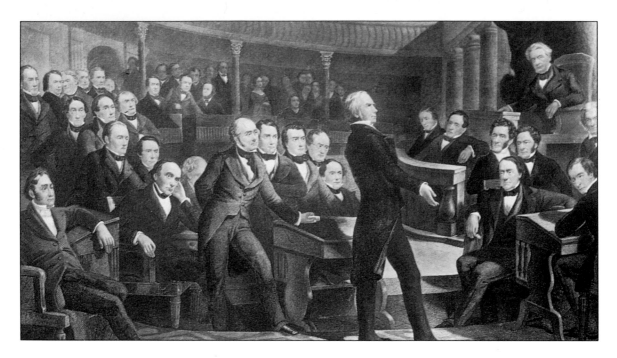

James Polk. Clay said of his three unsuccessful campaigns, "I would rather be right than be president."

Despite these losses, the Whigs finally won the presidency in 1848 by sending Zachary Taylor, who had spent much of his life in Kentucky, to the White House. Taylor was a war hero in the Mexican War (1846–48), a conflict arising from territorial disputes between Texas and Mexico.

By 1850, Kentucky's population was close to 1 million—four times what it was in 1800. Since the turn of the century several colleges had been founded to educate the increasing number of Kentuckians. In the 1820s and 1830s, colleges were started by Presbyterians, Baptists, Methodists, Catholics, and the Disciples of Christ. The University of Louisville, founded in 1798 as a seminary, became a college in 1837. It claims to be the oldest city university in the country.

Also in the 1830s, a close-knit religious group, or "sect," of people called the Shakers founded two communities in Kentucky. The Shakers did not believe in personal property, but instead shared all their possessions as a group. The rules of their community did not allow marriage or bearing children, although entire families— men, women, and children—often joined. In addition, Shaker communities sometimes took in orphans. The Shakers believed that all activities should be performed as a tribute to God—that a well-plowed field was as important as a well-written sermon.

Meanwhile, as the state's population and educational system grew, so did its economy. Small frontier farms expanded into large organizations that grew crops on a much larger scale. Kentucky became a leading producer of tobacco, corn, hemp, and flax. The state also supplied coal, iron, and distilled liquors throughout the region.

The Mississippi and Ohio rivers were the major trade and transportation routes. Once they reached the port of New Orleans, Kentucky products were shipped to the West Indies and as far away as Europe. But many areas still lacked a link to the river system, including Lexington, which couldn't ship goods by water. So in 1830, the state legislature voted to provide funds for a railroad to be built between Lexington and Louisville. The track was completed in 1852.

As Kentucky's economy grew with advances in transportation, manufacturing, and agriculture, it also continued to rely in part on slavery. The issue that people had argued over for most of the 19th century would soon be one they would kill and die over.

Kentucky statesman Henry Clay (opposite) was an important figure in the opening of the West. He twice served as Speaker of the House of Representatives, and was also secretary of state under President John Quincy Adams.

This sketch (below) shows a plan of the South Union Shaker community, one of two Shaker settlements in Kentucky. Organized in 1811, South Union was surrounded by land for farming and orchards, and contained mills, a meetinghouse, shops, and numerous "family" dwellings.

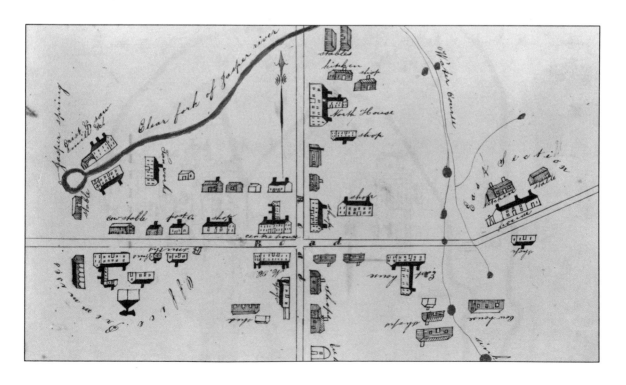

PART TWO

AN EVOLVING STATE

With access to both river and rail transport, Louisville became an important trade link between North and South. This 1876 view of Louisville shows a bustling city.

Through much of its history, Kentucky has been marked by both extreme wealth and extreme poverty. Kentucky's economy grew rapidly in the decades following the Civil War as its industries evolved and expanded. Horses, tobacco, whiskey, and coal all have become widely associated with the Bluegrass State. But new industries also brought problems and challenges for Kentuckians—especially coal mining, which took its toll not only on the environment but on the people working in the industry. Kentucky's challenges for the future include breaking the cycle of severe poverty that continues to affect many of its citizens and protecting its important natural resources.

Brother Against Brother

The Civil War finally broke out in 1861, although the issue of slavery had been threatening to tear the Union apart for years. Kentucky leaders such as Henry Clay played key roles in trying to work out a compromise between the two sides. But the issue of slavery and the right of individual states to set their own policies had turned out to be too controversial. After a certain point, compromise was no longer possible. Ultimately, the Southern states decided to withdraw from the Union and form their own nation, the Confederacy. The Northern states refused to allow this split, and civil war was the result.

Perhaps nowhere was the Civil War so divisive as it was in Kentucky. This was, after all, a state that produced both the leader of the Union, President Abraham Lincoln, and the leader of the Confederacy, Jefferson Davis. Kentuckians had family and business

Shown here in 1860, President Abraham Lincoln (above, right) is Kentucky's best-known native son. He was born in a log cabin in Hodgenville, Kentucky, but moved to Indiana with his family when he was seven years old.

Kentucky-born Jefferson Davis (right) considered himself more of a soldier than a politician and had not expected to be elected president of the Confederacy. He remained a staunch supporter of the Southern cause even after the war ended.

ties in both the North and the South. Large landowners in the Bluegrass Region depended on slavery to run their plantations, while many people throughout the state were strongly opposed to the practice of slavery.

As the debate over slavery and states' rights divided the Union, Henry Clay again helped settle the matter temporarily. Clay proposed what came to be called the Compromise of 1850. At the time, each new state to join the Union fueled debate in Congress over whether they should be allowed to keep slaves. Clay proposed admitting California as a free state and allowing Utah and New Mexico to practice slavery. His proposal passed in Congress after many stormy debates.

Clay's compromise mended the rift between North and South only temporarily. The Southern states ultimately withdrew from the Union and formed the Confederacy. When war between the North and the South erupted in April 1861, a divided Kentucky declared its neutrality, although the state government decreed that the state would not leave the Union. Kentucky's neutrality meant almost every community in the state could send men to fight for both sides.

Even prominent Kentucky families were divided. President Lincoln's wife, Mary Todd, came from a slave-owning Kentucky family, and many of her relatives fought with the Confederacy. Two of Senator John Crittenden's sons served as generals, one for the Union, and the other for the Confederacy. Of Henry Clay's five grandsons, three fought with the South and two with the North.

While Kentucky's neutral position kept the state from being a major focus of the bloodiest fighting, it was not enough to keep the war entirely outside of Kentucky's borders. Within months of the war's outbreak, the Confederates occupied eastern Kentucky, Bowling Green, and Columbus. Union forces quickly took control of Louisville and Paducah.

In September 1861, pro-North state legislators demanded that the Confederates leave Kentucky. But the state had plenty of Southern sympathizers, and they formed their own pro-Confederacy government with a capital in Bowling Green. The Rebels then accepted Kentucky as a Confederate state, although it wasn't long before Union troops drove out the Confederate government: Early in 1862, Confederate troops withdrew from Bowling Green.

In August, Southern forces won their first major victory in Kentucky when General Edmund Kirby Smith marched through the Cumberland Gap toward Lexington and defeated Union troops at Richmond. At the same time, Confederate general Braxton Bragg pushed through Nashville into Kentucky.

On their way into Kentucky's interior in October 1862, Bragg's men met Union troops led by General Don Carlos Buell at Perryville, near Harrodsburg. The men on both sides were unprepared for the battle that followed, the bloodiest in Kentucky history. Some 28,000 men fired at one another for hours. In the end, Bragg withdrew, but it was hardly a clear victory for the North: A total of nearly 7,700 men on both sides had been killed or wounded.

The Battle at Perryville was the last major Civil War battle in Kentucky, but Kentuckians continued to suffer from the effects of war. Many were victims in the often bloody raids that troops from both North and South conducted on Kentucky property. Confederate cavalry general and Kentucky native John Hunt Morgan was one of the most colorful raiders in the war. Often sporting feathers in his hat, Morgan repeatedly led his band of men, known as Morgan's Raiders, on daring raids into Union strongholds in Kentucky. The riders sought to stir up support for the South while also harassing Union troops.

Other raiders caused more direct harm against Kentucky residents and their property. Just about every county in the state suffered vicious attacks from raiding bands of one kind or another. Gangs of raiders descended on farms and communities, stealing livestock and valuables, and killing or wounding anyone who stood in their

The battle of Perryville on October 8, 1862, was the bloodiest Civil War battle to take place in Kentucky, with nearly 8,000 men killed. This illustration by William Delaney Travis shows a regiment of Union troops, on right, charging at Confederate soldiers.

way. Union leaders blamed the attacks on Confederates, while Confederates blamed them on Union troops. In many cases, the raiders had no ties to either side: Some were army deserters, others were simply taking advantage of the wartime disorder to seize property and goods for their own profit.

The Civil War had a huge and lasting impact on Kentucky. Roughly 140,000 Kentucky men fought in the war, and of these 40,000 fought for the South. The divisions caused by the conflict did not simply disappear at war's end; for many years, Kentuckians were faced with the challenges of recovering from the devastating effects of the war and adapting to a changing nation.

Reconstruction and Racial Conflict

Although Kentucky never officially pulled away from the Union during the Civil War, it still shared some of the South's pain in the Reconstruction years immediately following. These were troubled years for Kentuckians, who were still stinging from the war and the bitter splits it had caused throughout the state.

When the Civil War ended in 1865, the state remained under the tight control of the Union. Concerned about pro-South feelings in Kentucky, Lincoln had imposed tough restrictions on the state's residents by the war's end. Many Kentuckians resented the continued presence of Union soldiers long after the fighting was over. They also resented the way the North treated the conquered Southern states during the period known as Reconstruction. Kentuckians became more and more sympathetic to the South during this period.

The state's economy was in shambles. Crops and livestock had been badly depleted by the constant raids conducted during the war. Southern states could not afford many of Kentucky's farm products, especially hemp, a material used for making bags for cotton bales and ropes for sailing ships. Because of the tattered economy throughout the South, the amount of boat traffic along the Mississippi and Ohio rivers also dropped, almost paralyzing Kentucky's port cities.

One of the biggest challenges facing the state concerned the newly freed slaves. The fact that Kentucky had mixed feelings about slavery did not guarantee a smooth transition once the practice became illegal. And in the course of the war, many people in Kentucky changed their positions about slavery and the South. They resented the way the federal government had freed slaves without compensating the slave owners for lost property. As a result of these attitudes, newly freed slaves in Kentucky faced many obstacles as they tried to make new lives for themselves.

Former slaves had trouble finding jobs in cities and towns, and many of them had to continue working on plantations for wealthy whites, often for very little money—or none at all. Black Kentuckians also faced violence from the Ku Klux Klan, a group of former Confederates determined not to allow ex-slaves to have the same rights as white citizens. Often wearing white hoods and robes, these "Klansmen" attacked, terrorized, and murdered black citizens.

In 1866, the state legislature passed a law granting civil rights to African Americans, but without property and

education, many former slaves saw little improvement in their lives. That same year, the legislature set up schools to provide proper education to African Americans, but those schools usually had very small operating budgets.

Berea College, chartered in 1866, provided education to blacks and whites alike. But generally in Kentucky blacks and whites attended separate schools. In 1904, the state passed a law forbidding schools to educate blacks and whites together. As a result, even Berea was forced to segregate its students by building separate facilities for African Americans.

The Civil War tore apart many communities and caused ill feelings within many families. Much of this strife stemmed from the North-South divisions, and some of it resulted directly from the raids and general lawlessness that had plagued the state during the war. These tensions between Kentucky citizens did not disappear when the war ended. All across Kentucky, and especially in the rugged mountain regions, feuds roared on for years after the war. Many Kentuckians died in these feuds, paying the price for some grudge or past evil deed long since forgotten.

The most famous of these feuds pitted the McCoy family of Pike County, Kentucky, against the Hatfields of Mingo County, West Virginia. Exactly

how the feud began is uncertain, but it has become part of modern folklore. Some historians believe the grudge began in the Civil War, when most of the Hatfields supported the Confederates while most of the Mc-Coys supported the Union. Others argue it began after one of the Hatfields stole a hog belonging to the McCoy family in 1878.

Whatever the case, the families fought each other for decades. Separated by the Tug Fork River, they exchanged revenge attacks to avenge old wrongs. At least twelve people are known to have been killed in that feud, although some estimate the number to be much higher.

African-American families like the one shown in this photograph (opposite) saw little improvement in their living conditions after slavery was abolished in Kentucky in 1865. Black Kentuckians had few job or educational opportunities in the years following the Civil War.

This photograph (above) shows members of the Hatfield family of West Virginia, whose bitter and often violent feud with the McCoys of Kentucky may have resulted in more than twenty deaths, in separate incidents. Although the origin of the feud, which lasted for seventeen years, has become blurred over time, it is thought to have started over a stolen hog.

Bluegrass and Bourbon

Spurred on by technological advances in the course of the 19th century, America began to evolve into an industrialized nation. Factories sprang up throughout the country, especially in the Northeast, as manufacturing and mass production became key segments of the American economy. Kentucky remained largely an agricultural state, although some new industries developed in the late 19th century. The state government responded by investing in new roads and railway lines to help these industries expand.

Some Kentucky businesses, such as horse breeding and distilling bourbon whiskey, had been around for years. These expanded dramatically in the late 1800s. The custom of racing horses in contests became so popular that the trend carried over into town streets. In 1810 the state was forced to ban this dangerous practice.

As horse racing gained in popularity, the breeding of racehorses became an industry in its own right. Kentucky's Bluegrass Region near Lexington developed a strong reputation for producing outstanding racehorses. To this day, breeders boast that something in the rare variety of grass there produces stronger and faster horses.

Following the Civil War, the horse-breeding industry grew dramatically. Wealthy Easterners took a strong interest in buying horses from the

famed Bluegrass Region, and Kentuckians themselves were breeding and racing their own horses. As a result, many horse farms and stables opened in the Bluegrass Region in the second half of the 19th century.

On May 17, 1875, a chestnut-colored colt named Aristides beat thirteen other thoroughbreds on a new racetrack in Louisville called Churchill Downs. African-American jockey Oliver Lewis rode Aristides to win the very first Kentucky Derby, a race that has become America's most famous thoroughbred event.

Another traditional Kentucky art, distilling bourbon whiskey, turned into big business following the Civil War. Demand for bourbon from soldiers on both sides soared during the war. What had been a sideline for farmers and families turned into a booming business, and the number of bourbon distilleries across the state rapidly multiplied.

But as the success of Kentucky whiskey grew, so did public opposition to it. Many people were aware of the problems caused by alcohol and drunkenness. The temperance movement sought to make the selling and drinking of alcohol illegal. The movement had many supporters in Kentucky and across the country, and it eventually succeeded in passing an amendment to the U.S. Constitution that outlawed alcohol in 1919. But decades earlier, Kentucky state leaders had passed their own restrictions pro-

The popularity of Kentucky bourbon did not prevent a group of 19th-century women and clergymen from trying to make alcohol consumption illegal. This 1874 cartoon (above) shows a young woman in armor destroying barrels of alcohol. The leg of a fleeing man can be seen at lower right.

Rich in lime, the grass of Kentucky's Bluegrass Region is said to be largely responsible for the strong racehorses produced in Kentucky. French artist Edward Troye spent a great deal of time in the Bluegrass State creating paintings of horses, including this one (opposite).

hibiting citizens in many areas of Kentucky from buying alcohol legally—even though the state had become famous for its bourbon. To this day, many counties remain "dry," meaning they do not allow the sale or drinking of alcohol.

Politics were often volatile during

this period, and Kentucky ushered in the 20th century with one of the most shocking events in its political history. In the 1899 race for governor, Republican William S. Taylor beat William Goebel, his Democratic opponent, in a close election. The Democrats accused the Republicans of cheating in the election and demanded a re-count. On January 30, 1900, Goebel was assasinated by an unknown gunman. Before he died, the legislature declared him the winner, and Goebel's running mate, J.C.W. Beckham, became governor.

Both Republicans and Democrats were committed to helping Kentucky's economy expand. One of the most important factors in improving the state's economy was the amount of money the state poured into upgrading its land transportation network during the late 1800s and early 1900s. These finances paid for a road network that farmers and industries could use to transport their goods to cities and ports. Private companies owned and maintained many of the state's roads once they were built. They charged toll fees, and as the road conditions worsened the tolls were increased to pay for repairs.

Most citizens relied on horse and wagon for travel (automobiles were still scarce at this point). Travelers resented the high fees they had to pay to travel in their state. By the late 1890s, many citizens protested by tearing down the toll gates across the roads. In what came to be called the Toll Gate War, violent raids against the toll keepers finally forced the state to take over the highways. Kentucky created a department of public roads in 1912 and a few years later started building a state highway system.

The Toll Gate War was just one example of violent protest in Kentucky during this period. The farming community also had troubles, especially after Kentucky farmers discovered they could grow burley tobacco, replacing hemp as a major cash crop. Kentucky's soil turned out to be just right for growing this milder tobacco, which by 1890 had become the state's biggest crop. Then, a group of tobacco companies banded together to buy up most of the state's tobacco, completely changing Kentucky's tobacco market by 1900. The companies could buy tobacco without competition from other buyers, and farmers saw prices for their produce drop dramatically.

Kentucky tobacco farmers joined together in protest. Many of them teamed up and kept their crops in storage until they could receive better prices. Other farmers, who could not afford to keep their tobacco in storage, decided not to join these protestors and continued dealing with the large companies. Tensions between both groups of farmers exploded in 1904, when the Tobacco War (also known as the Black Patch War) broke out. For five years, there was lawless-

Kentucky's tobacco industry started growing dramatically in the late 19th century. Buyers from all over the world bid on Kentucky's tobacco harvest at auctions such as the one shown in this scene (above).

This advertisement (right) uses people's fascination with the rugged, exciting lives of Kentucky's pioneers to sell tobacco.

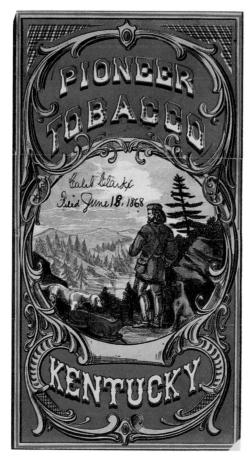

ness and bloodshed in the tobacco farm region as night riders banded together and raided farms and warehouses.

Using similar tactics as the Ku Klux Klan, these masked night riders destroyed tobacco fields and burned down warehouses to hurt the tobacco trusts and those farmers selling to them. Finally, Governor Augustus Willson called in the state troops, hoping to put an end to the raids. In the end, the farmers' violent revolution resulted in a fairer market system for tobacco farmers. Tobacco was now sold at auctions through open bidding, leading to better prices for the farmers.

By the start of the 20th century, coal mining, another important—although troubled—industry had grown extensively in Kentucky. The state has always had a large supply of coal, both in the western and eastern parts of Kentucky, but coal did not play a major role in the state's economy until the early 20th century when rich underground supplies of coal were discovered in the east. Coal was used throughout the country to heat homes and fuel factories. Northern corporations built railroads to reach the coal supplies in eastern Kentucky, and as mining techniques improved, the state supplied the nation with more and more coal.

The mining industry provided jobs for thousands of people, but it was difficult work. Miners suffered tough

Kentucky coal miners were lowered to the mine shafts in elevators. The elevators descended 1,550 feet in less than a minute, and the only illumination came from the candle lamps that the miners carried.

and dangerous working conditions. Men worked long hours in dark, cramped caves, facing the constant threat of a cave-in or an explosion. Many were killed or disabled on the job. Those who managed to avoid such accidents often became sick with incurable lung disease from breathing coal dust for so many years.

The mining industry would have a major impact on Kentucky citizens throughout the 20th century, as the nation's demand for coal increased and fell.

Bad Times,
War Times

Kentucky, like the nation, saw its fortunes rise and fall during the first half of the 20th century. Two world wars, labor struggles, economic catastrophe, and boom times all had a great impact during this period.

Kentucky played an important role when America entered World War I in 1917, which was being fought thousands of miles away in France and Germany. About 80,000 Kentucky soldiers were trained at four state training camps to fight for America during the war.

The war also led to increased demand for timber and coal, and many Kentuckians sold their land to out-of-state companies for a profit. The timber and coal boom provided thousands of jobs, which in turn helped the state's economy. Along with the jobs, however, came problems. Loggers cut down hundreds of thousands of acres of centuries-old woodlands to meet the demand for timber. As sawmills sprang up across

There were four military training camps in Kentucky during World War I. The soldiers shown in this photograph, at Camp Zachary Taylor near Louisville, had a rigorous training schedule that included early-morning calisthenics (stretching exercises).

the state, few people gave any thought to forest preservation or planting trees to replace those cut down. Eventually, many lumber communities ran out of timber. Jobs were lost and acres of cleared forests remained bare. It was not until the 1930s that the state began educating citizens about land management and reforestation, the practice of replanting trees.

The coal-mining boom brought more income to many of the Appalachian people, and it dramatically changed the way they lived. The mining companies built towns to house miners. In the early days of mining, the houses were often nicer than anyplace most workers had ever lived. As time went on, however, living conditions became worse, and miners and their families were crowded in rickety shacks without plumbing. Without their own small farms, miners were forced to buy food and household supplies at stores run by their employers, who charged high prices because the miners had nowhere else to go.

Songwriter Merle Travis wrote this famous song about his father, a coal miner who had to dig a great deal of coal every day for wages that went straight to the company store:

*You load sixteen tons and what do
    you get?*
*Another day older and deeper
    in debt.*
*Saint Peter, don't you call me 'cause
    I can't go,*
I owe my soul to the company store.

When the war ended, so did the coal mining boom. Many of the miners lost their jobs during the 1920s or had to take pay cuts. Those who had sold their land had little to show for years of hard labor.

When America's Great Depression hit in 1929, frustrated miners began organizing into labor unions. They demanded better working conditions and pay from the mining companies. The companies, however, resisted the union organizing efforts, and violence erupted as strikers and strikebreakers fought one another. The fights were so bitter that one southeastern Kentucky county came to be known across the country as "bloody Harlan County."

The labor union movement grew across the country during the 1930s,

As mining techniques and equipment improved, so did production. By 1920, Kentucky was producing nearly 39 million tons of coal a year. A miner in Hopkins County, Kentucky, uses a hand-operated mining drill to extract coal from an underground mine (opposite).

Miners, like this one (above) in Harlan County preparing to go home at the end of a long day, worked in difficult conditions and often for little pay. Many of them looked to their unions for help in improving conditions.

and Kentuckians played an active role. In 1938, an agreement signed between the United Mine Workers of America and the coal mining companies finally led to higher wages and improved working conditions.

One industry that did not prosper during the war years was whiskey distilling. In 1919, Congress passed and the states ratified the 18th Amendment to the U.S. Constitution, making the sale and manufacture of alcohol illegal.

Some distillers retired from the whiskey business and tried to make a living growing traditional crops such as tobacco. Others struggled to make money producing vinegar or types of whiskey the government recognized as medicine. Still others continued to operate "moonshine" stills illegally—a profitable business, since alcohol was getting harder and harder to find but remained in high demand. Authorities known as revenue officers searched Kentucky's backwoods during this period looking for illegal whiskey operations. In 1933, Congress passed and the states ratified the 21st Amendment ending Prohibition—people could once again sell alcohol legally, and Kentucky was free to resume its profitable distilling industry.

The Depression caused severe poverty in Kentucky just as it did across the country. In an effort to put Americans back to work, President Franklin Delano Roosevelt created "New Deal" government programs. The Works Progress Administration (WPA) and Public Works Administration (PWA) not only created jobs, but also built roads and schools. In 1936, the federal government built the nation's gold vault at Fort Knox, south of Louisville, which it still uses to store billions of dollars worth of gold. Government-funded adult education programs helped teach poorly educated Kentuckians important skills such as reading and writing. More employment and educational opportunities meant that fewer people had to rely on farming to make a living.

World War II yanked the country out of its economic depression. America entered the war abroad after the Japanese bombed Pearl Harbor in 1941. Nearly 306,000 people from Kentucky, both men and women, served their country, and close to 8,000 were killed during the war.

The need for war supplies charged up the country's industries, and Kentucky was no exception. Again, demand soared for coal to fuel factories supplying goods for the war effort. Farmers benefited from the army's demand for Kentucky's agricultural products.

When World War II broke out, thousands of soldiers trained at camps such as Fort Knox, Kentucky. Pictured here (above, right) are armored cars, which were able to move rapidly over rough terrain and could transport soldiers easily.

This photograph (right) of Knox County farmers plowing with oxen in the 1940s shows how little some agricultural practices had changed since the state's pioneer days.

Growth and New Challenges

Kentucky entered a new era following World War II. The manufacturing boom that began during the war continued, replacing farming as a primary way of life for most Kentuckians. Factories producing everything from clothing to whiskey to machinery became major employers during the postwar years. Especially in the Ohio Valley, Kentucky industries that manufactured chemicals, industrial parts, automobiles, and electrical supplies all prospered during this time.

As manufacturing took off, people came in from the country in search of better opportunities and the population of Kentucky's cities grew. Even as the number of farmers in Kentucky diminished, however, agricultural production improved. Machines helped farmers harvest more crops in less time. Also, experts helped farmers keep their land productive by teaching them how to avoid erosion and other farming problems, and plant scientists came up with new varieties of crops that produced much bigger harvests.

Rural Kentuckians saw big changes in their lives following the war. The job-producing programs that began during the Depression provided electricity to even the most distant sections of the state. Radio and television brought information that connected Kentucky to the rest of the country.

Four-lane interstate highways opened, filling an important gap in the country's transportation system.

The tourism industry also began to blossom after the war. With a growing system of scenic and historical parks, the state began attracting visitors from all over the world.

The decades following World War II included the completion of some major public projects: an atomic energy plant near Paducah in 1953, a massive dam project in western Kentucky in 1964, and a huge steam-generating plant at Paradise in 1969. The dams, built by the Tennessee Valley Authority, created two lakes with a peninsula between them. The area, called the Land Between the Lakes, became one of Kentucky's most popular vacation areas.

For all the progress, the state still had to grapple with nationwide changes. Throughout the first half of the 20th century, for instance, Kentucky's education system prohibited white and black students from attend-

The Kentucky Dam (opposite, top), completed by the Tennessee Valley Authority in 1944, not only generates electricity but helps regulate flooding along the lower Ohio and Mississippi rivers. It is located in Kentucky near the mouth of the Tennessee River.

The Land Between the Lakes (right), completed in 1964, is a popular Kentucky recreation and conservation area. This tourist destination consists of a reservoir—created by the damming project—divided into two lakes by a 270,000-acre strip of land.

ing school together. That segregation was challenged in 1948 when a federal court in Lexington ordered the University of Kentucky to admit black students. It was a great victory for African Americans, who had been trying to break down the state's segregation barriers for years.

In 1954, the U.S. Supreme Court took on the issue of segregation in the historic case *Brown* v. *Board of Education*. The Supreme Court ruled that the practice of school segregation was unconstitutional at all levels. Unlike many Southern governors, Kentucky governor Lawrence Wetherby immediately agreed to follow the Supreme Court's order.

In 1964, Kentucky's general assembly debated whether to pass a law against racial discrimination. The Reverend Martin Luther King, Jr., visited Frankfort and led a march supporting the law. Some of the marchers took part in a five-day hunger strike. The legislature still did not pass the law, but Governor Edward Breathitt met with the hunger strikers and promised to support their efforts. In 1966, Kentucky became the first Southern state to pass a strong civil rights law, which outlawed discrimination of employees and patrons of hotels and motels.

Concern about the environment also increased in the 1960s. Environmental problems stemmed both from old Kentucky industries, such as mining, and new industrial businesses. One of the biggest debates concerned

the practice of strip mining. Rather than digging tunnels or shafts in a mountain, this method uses heavy machinery to strip off the tops of mountains and hills to reach veins of coal. The practice makes coal mining much cheaper, but leaves ugly, barren land where forests and farms used to be. It also causes problems such as soil erosion and mud slides, which clog streams and rivers.

In 1966, the state passed a conservation law restricting strip mining, but the law said nothing about repairing the damage caused by this destructive mining technique. In 1978, a federal law went into effect requiring mine owners to reclaim, or repair, the stripped land. The process involves filling in, irrigating, and replanting the scarred property.

Kentuckians have also become increasingly concerned about proper disposal of industrial waste. Without laws to stop the practice, industries outside the state often ship their dangerous waste materials to Kentucky, especially to the industrialized Louisville area. One of the most shocking incidents occurred in the late 1960s, when an illegal dump containing tens of thousands of drums of industrial waste was discovered on a farm near Louisville. The Valley of the Drums, as it was called, shocked the nation and pushed Congress to start its Superfund program. The program selects the nation's most polluted sites for expensive cleanup efforts.

Strip mining has a devastating effect on land— this rocky, eroded patch of land (opposite) was once fertile forestland. In order to control the practice, Kentucky passed stricter laws that require mining companies to restore the land in mined areas.

Louisville native Muhammad Ali (above), born Cassius Clay, became one of the most celebrated boxers in the sport's history, holding the world heavyweight title for four straight years.

The Next Chapter

By 1980, Kentucky had changed greatly since World War II. Cities, and especially suburbs, had grown dramatically. A modern road network had been laid down to bring commuters to the state's industrial centers and to make the state accessible to tourists.

Today, tourism is an important part of Kentucky's economy. Visitors and residents can enjoy many attractions, such as museums; theater, and music performances; state parks that offer everything from unusual caves and beautiful lakes to historic landmarks; and Kentucky's many equestrian events, including the world-famous Kentucky Derby.

As the end of the 20th century approaches, social scientists talk about "the New South," referring to the region's growing importance to the country's economy, and an area where more and more people and businesses want to locate. Kentucky, with its rich supply of natural resources and its diversified economy, is at the forefront of this New South. This became especially clear in 1986, when Toyota Motors chose Georgetown, Kentucky, as the best place to build an $800 million car assembly plant. While other areas of America faced increasing economic problems, the Toyota plant in Kentucky created thousands of skilled labor jobs and led to the opening of dozens of new related businesses.

Other automobile plants have opened in the state recently: Ford has a plant in Louisville, and the makers of the Corvette automobile have opened a facility in Bowling Green.

Economic advancement requires properly educated citizens, however, and Kentucky had long fallen short in that area. As of 1990, one in three adult Kentuckians had not graduated from high school—one of the worst graduation rates in the country.

But the state finally responded aggressively to education problems in 1990 by approving one of the nation's most dramatic and ambitious plans for reforming its school system. The Kentucky Supreme Court declared the entire school system unconstitutional

The Kentucky Derby (opposite), held each May at Louisville's Churchill Downs, remains the most famous annual event in Kentucky.

When Toyota Motors selected Kentucky for the site of a new manufacturing plant (above), the decision not only created 4,500 new jobs at the plant, but also encouraged the growth of many small businesses. Within a few years, Toyota had brought nearly 18,000 job opportunities to the area.

because property taxes were unfairly distributed to the state's school districts. This system meant that rich areas had more money to spend on education than poorer communities.

But the state did more than just change the way school districts receive money. Kentucky changed the entire system. It turned most of the educational and administrative decisions over to the local school districts. The argument was that local schools are better equipped than the state government to teach local children. Kentucky's education reform effort has become a model for the entire nation.

The state still must overcome major challenges, however. As economic development improves the lives of thousands of Kentuckians, many others continue to live in extreme poverty. Those people who can't find jobs depend on government programs to pay for food and housing. Solving the problems of rural poverty is perhaps the greatest challenge Kentucky faces in its future.

Even as Kentuckians grapple with a poor education system, land planning efforts, and pollution control, the future looks promising. Kentucky's natural resources, its strong appeal to tourists, and its improving economy could make the state economically vital in the next century. The fact that the state is confronting severe problems head-on is a good sign—throughout Kentucky's history, many rugged individuals have overcome hardships and challenges. That spirit must continue if the state is going to thrive in a rapidly changing world.

This photograph shows a nighttime view of Louisville's modern skyline. The genteel style of old Louisville remains, but today the city is a cosmopolitan metropolis that attracts thousands of visitors each year.

Land area:
    39,732 square miles, including 679
    square miles of inland water. Ranks 37th
    in size.

Major rivers:
    The Ohio; the Kentucky; the Big Sandy;
    the Licking; the Green; the Cumberland;
    the Tennessee; the Mississippi.

Highest point: Black Mountain, 4,145 ft.

Climate:
    Average January temperature: 32F°
    Average July temperature: 76F°

Major bodies of water:
    Kentucky Lake; Lake Cumberland; Cave
    Run Lake; Green River Lake; Greenbo
    Lake; Rough River Lake; Dale Hallow
    Reservoir; Lake Barkley.

Population: 3,754,715 (1992)
Rank: 23rd
 1900: 2,147,000
 1790: 74,000

Population of major cities (1993):
Louisville	269,555
Lexington	225,366
Bowling Green	40,688
Hopkinsville	29,818
Paducah	27,256
Frankfort	26,535

Ethnic breakdown by percentage (1990):
White	91.7%
Hispanic	0.6 %
African American	7.1 %
Asian	0.5 %
American Indian	0.1 %
Other	0.03%

Economy:
 Coal mining, insurance, transportation, real estate, agriculture (tobacco, soybeans, corn, cattle), horses, manufacturing (electronics, automobiles, whiskey, cigarettes), tourism, retail, and construction.

State government:
 Legislature: Made up of a 38-member Senate and a 100-member House. Senators serve 4-year terms, representatives serve 2-year terms.
 Governor: The governor is chief executive of the state and is elected to serve a 4-year term.
 Courts: Kentucky's judicial branch has 4 levels; district and circuit courts in each county, the court of appeals, and the supreme court.
State capital: Frankfort

State Flag

The Kentucky flag shows the state seal against a blue field with the title "Commonwealth of Kentucky" wrapping around the top. It was adopted in 1928.

State Seal

Kentucky's seal, adopted in 1792, salutes friendship and unity. Two men clasp hands, encircled by the state motto and two sprigs of goldenrod, the state flower.

State Motto

Kentucky's motto, "United we stand, divided we fall," is believed to be from "The Liberty Song," popular during the Revolutionary War.

State Nickname

"The Bluegrass State" refers to the bluegrass that grows in Kentucky's rich soil. The grass is actually green, but in the spring it produces blue buds.

Places

Abraham Lincoln Birthplace, Hodgenville

American Printing House for the Blind, Louisville

Appalachian Museum, Berea

Ardsmore House Museum, Princeton

Ashland, Henry Clay's homestead, Lexington

Big South Fork National River, Big South Fork

Blue Heron Mining Community, Big South Fork

Blue Licks Battlefield, Blue Licks Springs

Calumet Horse Farm, Lexington

Childhood home of Mary Todd Lincoln, Lexington

Churchill Downs, Louisville

Colonel Harland Sanders Museum, Louisville

Cumberland Gap National Historic Park, Middlesboro

Daniel Boone National Forest, near Hazard

Duncan House Museum, Greenville

Frank Lloyd Wright's Zeigler House, Frankfort

George Rogers Clark Memorial, Harrodsburg

Indian burial grounds, Wickliffe

Jefferson Davis Monument, Fairview

John James Audubon Museum and State Park, Henderson

to See

Kentucky History Museum, Frankfort

Kentucky Horse Park, Iron Works Pike

Kentucky Derby Museum, Louisville

Louisville Zoo, Louisville

Lexington Children's Museum, Lexington

Lincoln's Boyhood Home, Hodgenville

Lincoln Museum, Hodgenville

Luscher's Museum of the American Farmer, Frankfort

Mammoth Cave National Park, Cave City

Museum of American Quilters Society, Paducah

Museum of History and Science, Louisville

Natural Bridge State Park, Slade

Oscar Gatz Whiskey History Museum, Bardstown

Perryville Battlefield State Shrine, Perryville

Robert Penn Warren Birthplace Museum, Guthrie

Shaker Village, Pleasant Hill

St. Joseph's Cathedral, Bardstown

Stephen Collins Foster Memorial, Bardstown

Toyota Manufacturing Plant, Georgetown

Trail of Tears Commemorative State Park, Hopkinsville

U.S. Gold Depository, Fort Knox

State Flower

Goldenrod was adopted as Kentucky's state flower in 1926. The bright yellow wildflowers grow throughout the state.

State Bird

Adopted in 1926 as the state bird, the Kentucky cardinal makes its home in Kentucky's fields and woods year-round.

State Tree

In 1994, Kentucky's legislature chose the tulip poplar as the state tree, to replace the Kentucky coffee tree. The tulip poplar has a tall, straight trunk and broad, dark-green leaves.

Kentucky History

1654 Col. Abraham Wood explores what is now Kentucky

1682 Robert Cavalier, Sieur de La Salle, claims the Mississippi Valley for France

1736 French traders establish first village along the Ohio River in Kentucky

1750 Thomas Walker of Virginia discovers the Cumberland Gap

1769 Daniel Boone arrives in Kentucky

1774 James Harrod founds Harrodsburg, first permanent settlement in Kentucky

1775 Daniel Boone blazes the Wilderness Trail and starts building Fort Boonesborough

1776 Kentucky County is created as part of Virginia

1778 Louisville is founded

1782 Kentucky force is defeated in Battle of Blue Licks

1786 Virginia General Assembly releases Kentucky as a Virginia county; process toward statehood begins

1792 Kentucky becomes 15th state

1811 First steamboat arrives at Falls of Ohio

1830 First railroad construction begins in the state

1849 Third state constitution is adopted

1855 "Bloody Monday" riots erupt in Louisville

American

1492 Christopher Columbus reaches the New World

1607 Jamestown (Virginia) founded by English colonists

1620 *Mayflower* arrives at Plymouth (Massachusetts)

1754–63 French and Indian War

1765 Parliament passes Stamp Act

1775–83 Revolutionary War

1776 Signing of the Declaration of Independence

1788–90 First congressional elections

1791 Bill of Rights added to U.S. Constitution

1803 Louisiana Purchase

1812–14 War of 1812

1820 Missouri Compromise

1836 Battle of the Alamo, Texas

1846–48 Mexican-American War

1849 California Gold Rush

1860 South Carolina secedes from Union

1861–65 Civil War

1862 Lincoln signs Homestead Act

1863 Emancipation Proclamation

1865 President Lincoln assassinated (April 14)

1865–77 Reconstruction in the South

1866 Civil Rights bill passed

1881 President James Garfield shot (July 2)

History

1896 First Ford automobile is made

1898–99 Spanish-American War

1901 President William McKinley is shot (Sept. 6)

1917 U.S. enters World War I

1922 Nineteenth Amendment passed, giving women the vote

1929 U.S. stock market crash; Great Depression begins

1933 Franklin D. Roosevelt becomes president; begins New Deal

1941 Japanese attack Pearl Harbor (Dec. 7); U.S. enters World War II

1945 U.S. drops atomic bomb on Hiroshima and Nagasaki; Japan surrenders, ending World War II

1963 President Kennedy assassinated (November 22)

1964 Civil Rights Act passed

1965–73 Vietnam War

1968 Martin Luther King, Jr., shot in Memphis (April 4)

1974 President Richard Nixon resigns because of Watergate scandal

1979–81 Hostage crisis in Iran: 52 Americans held captive for 444 days

1989 End of U.S.-Soviet cold war

1991 Gulf War

1993 U.S. signs North American Free Trade Agreement with Canada and Mexico

Kentucky History

1861 Kentucky declares neutrality in Civil War

1865 University of Kentucky is founded

1866 First bridge built across the Ohio River

1875 Aristedes wins first Kentucky Derby

1882 Hatfield-McCoy feud starts

1891 Present state constitution is adopted

1900 William Goebel, candidate for governor, is killed

1905–09 "Tobacco War" rages in western Kentucky

1914 State legislature approves statewide road network

1936 U.S. Treasury establishes a gold vault at Fort Knox

1944 Kentucky Dam built, creating Kentucky Lake

1948 University of Kentucky opens to black students

1955 Voting age for state elections changed from 21 to 18

1983 Martha Layne Collins elected first woman governor in state history

1986 Toyota builds new assembly plant in Kentucky

1990 Statewide education reform begins

1994 Voters in Kentucky's 2nd District elect a Republican to U.S. Congress for the first time since the Civil War

Thomas Walker (1715–94)
A Virginia surveyor, Walker led the first documented expedition through the Cumberland Gap.

Daniel Boone (1734–1820)
This frontiersman from North Carolina blazed the Wilderness Road through the Cumberland Gap all the way to the Kentucky River. He founded Fort Boonesborough.

John Fitch (1743–98) A native of Connecticut and long-time Kentucky resident, this inventor conceived the idea for the steamboat in 1785 and received the first patent for it in 1791.

George Rogers Clark (1752–1818) This explorer from Virginia was a frontier-general in the American Revolution and founded Louisville.

Henry Clay (1777–1852)
Known as "the great compromiser," Clay represented Kentucky in Congress, serving in both the House and the Senate. He was also a founder of the Whig party. Clay unsuccessfully tried to run for president three times.

Zachary Taylor (1784–1850)
This Mexican War hero grew up near Louisville and became the twelfth president of the U.S. in 1849. He died in office the following year.

John James Audubon (1785–1851) This artist and naturalist wrote and illustrated *The Birds of America*. Audubon lived in Kentucky from 1807 to 1820.

Mary Todd Lincoln

Jefferson Davis (1808–89)
A Kentucky native and a member of the U.S. Senate, Davis became the only president of the Confederate States of America.

Abraham Lincoln (1809–65) Born in a log cabin in Hodgenville, Lincoln grew up to become the six-teenth president of the United States. During his term (1861–65) he guided the country through the Civil War. Lincoln issued the Emancipation Proclamation to free slaves in 1862.

Cassius Clay (1810–1903)
Clay was a diplomat and well-known opponent of slavery who published *The True American*, an abolitionist newspaper in Lexington.

William Wells Brown (1815–84) Born a slave in Lexington, Wells wrote novels, drama, and history. He became the first African American to publish a novel with his book, *Clotel*.

Mary Todd Lincoln (1818–82) Born in Lexington, Mary Todd married Abraham Lincoln in 1842. She was First Lady from 1861 to 1865, when her husband was assassinated.

Adlai E. Stevenson (1835–1914) This Christian County native served as vice president under Grover Cleveland.

Carrie M. Nation (1846–1911) A crusader

against alcohol, Nation was born in Gerrard County. She traveled the country speaking publicly for temperance.

Daniel Carter Beard (1850–1941) Educated in Covington, Kentucky, Beard founded the Boy Scouts of America in 1910.

Louis Brandeis (1856–1941) The first Jew to sit on the U.S. Supreme Court, Louisville-born Brandeis was noted for his support of civil liberties and social welfare legislation.

Sophonisba Preston Breckinridge (1866–1948) Breckinridge, born in Lexington, was the first woman to be admitted to the Kentucky bar, as well as the first woman in the world to receive a Ph.D. in political science.

Thomas Hunt Morgan (1866–1945) This scientist from Lexington won the Nobel Prize for medicine in 1933 for his work in genetic research.

Alben W. Barkley (1877–1956) The son of a poor farmer in Graves County, Barkley served in both branches of Congress. He was also vice president under Harry Truman.

Col. Harland Sanders (1890–1980) Famous as "the Colonel," Sanders ran a cafe in Corbin well known for its fried chicken. He went on to found the Kentucky Fried Chicken restaurant chain in 1939.

Robert Penn Warren (1905–89) Born in Guthrie, this novelist and poet was a three-time Pulitzer Prize winner, whose works include *All the King's Men*.

Man O'War (1917–47) Known as "Big Red" for his size and chestnut coloring, Man O'War was one of the greatest horses to ever race in Kentucky. He won twenty out of twenty-one races before retiring.

Whitney M. Young, Jr. (1921–71) This Kentucky native served as director of the National Urban League from 1961 to 1971. In 1969, this civil rights leader was awarded the Medal of Freedom.

Franklin R. Sousley (1925–45) This World War II soldier, born in Kentucky, helped raise the flag at Iwo Jima and is pictured in one of the most famous war photographs in history.

Robert Penn Warren

Moneta J. Sleet, Jr. (b. 1926) Born in Owensboro, Kentucky, Sleet worked as a reporter and photographer and in 1969 became the first black American to win the Pulitzer Prize for feature photography.

Loretta Lynn (b. 1935) Born in Butcher Hollow, Lynn grew up to become a successful country music star, often singing about her childhood in Kentucky. Her records have sold millions, and her autobiography, *Coal Miner's Daughter*, was made into a popular motion picture.

Muhammed Ali (b. 1942) Born Cassius Marcellus Clay, Jr., in Louisville, this heavyweight fighter became an international boxing legend.

RESOURCE GUIDE

Pictures in this volume:

Keeneland Association: 50

Dover: 9 (top), 19, 25 (bottom), 40

Kentucky Department of Tourism: 53

Kentucky Historical Society: 30, 41, 42

Kentucky Resources & Environmental Protection Cabinet: 48

Library of Congress: 9, 11 (top), 12, 15 (both), 17 (both), 18, 21, 22, 23, 25 (top), 26, 27, 28, 29 (top), 37, 39 (both), 45 (top), 60

Media Projects Inc.: 29

National Archives: 43, 47 (top)

National Park Service: 7

Private Collection: 36

Smithsonian: 32

Tennessee Valley Administration: 47 (bottom)

Transylvania University Library: 34, 45 (bottom)

Toyota Motor Manufacturing USA: 51

West Virginia Division of Culture & History: 35

About the authors:

Katherine Snow Smith is a freelance writer and reporter with the *Tampa Bay Business Journal* in Florida. A native of Raleigh, NC, she graduated from the University of North Carolina at Chapel Hill with a Journalism degree and has worked at several newspapers.

Adam Smith is a reporter for the *St. Petersburg Times* in Florida, where he writes about government and politics. A graduate of Kenyon College in Ohio, he has worked for newspapers in Connecticut and South Carolina and now lives in Tampa, Florida.

Suggested reading:

Carpenter, Allan. *The New Enchantment of America: Kentucky.* Chicago: Childrens Press, 1979.

Dunnigan, Alice A. *The Fascinating Story of Black Kentuckians: Their Heritage and Tradition.* New York: Associated Features, Inc., 1990.

Fradin, Dennis B. *From Sea to Shining Sea: Kentucky.* Chicago: Childrens Press, 1993.

Hargrove, Jim. *Daniel Boone: Pioneer Trailblazer.* Chicago: Childrens Press, 1985.

Klotter, James C. *Our Kentucky: A Study of the Bluegrass State.* Lexington, KY: The University Press of Kentucky, 1992.

Lawlor, Laurie. *Daniel Boone.* Morton Grove, IL: Albert Whitman & Co., 1989.

Marsh, Carole. *Kentucky Jeopardy!: Answers and Questions about Our State!* Decatur, GA: Gallopade Publishing Group, 1991.

Marsh, Carole. *Kentucky Timeline: A Chronology of Kentucky History, Mystery, Trivia, Legend, Lore and More.* Decatur, GA: Gallopade Publishing Group, 1992.

For more information contact:

Kentucky Historical Society
PO Box H
Frankfort, KY 40602
(502) 564-3016

Kentucky Department of Travel Development
Capital Plaza Tower
Suite 2200
500 Metro Street
Frankfort, KY 40601-1968
(502) 564-4930

INDEX

Page numbers in *italics* indicate illustrations